The Twenty-Two Keys of the Tarot

Arland Ussher

The twenty-two keys of the Tarot

the designs drawn by
Leslie Mac Weeney

The Dolmen Press

*Set in Times Roman type with Goudy text
display and printed and published
in the Republic of Ireland
at the Dolmen Press,
North Richmond Industrial Estate,
North Richmond Street, Dublin 1*

*First published 1953
Second printing, reset, 1969
Third printing, 1970
This edition, reset, 1976*

*Distributed in the U.S.A. and in Canada by
Humanities Press Inc.,
171 First Avenue,
Atlantic Highlands,
N.J. 07716*

ISBN 0 85105 297 5 *paperback*
ISBN 0 85105 305 X *hardback*

Preface

The Tarot, the gift to Europe of Gypsies or returning Crusaders in the 14th century, belongs to the historic puzzles — the more as it cannot be distinctly traced in other continents. Together with the twenty-two picture-cards (which alone concern us here), a Tarot pack contains fifty-six 'pip-cards', corresponding to those of other packs; with the addition of a fourth court-card, the Knight, in each suit — suggesting a link with chess. The suits are known as Sceptres (or Wands), Swords, Cups and Coins or 'Pentacles' (in Germany, as Acorns, Leaves, Hearts and Bells); and upon this basis, 17th century French card-makers elaborated our familiar cards. These fifty-six pip-cards have always been used for play. The twenty-two 'Major Trumps', so-called, are ill-adapted however for this purpose, and in some countries are entirely omitted from Tarot sets. It seems natural therefore to connect their origin with divination (the fortune-telling traditionally associated with the Gypsies), with techniques of meditation (their affinity with Jung's archetypes is evident), and even (though this is mere conjecture) with the grades of initiation in the ancient Mysteries. There is a legend that a certain Pharaoh, wishing to preserve the ancestral wisdom in a time of war, planned to confide it to the most virtuous persons in his realm; whereupon some shrewd counsellor objected, 'If you intend that a thing shall last for ever, do not commit it into the hands of Virtue but into those of Vice'. Whether or not this was in fact the origin of the Tarot, it must be said that Vice has preserved the heritage little better than Virtue could have done; and a good Tarot set (such as the Marseilles Tarot, which we reproduce) is now very hard to come by. The correspondences here suggested with the Germanic runes are wholly my own; though I am indebted to my friend Baron von Metzradt for all I know about Runic. The Hebrew and Zodiacal attributions are those of the 19th century writers on Tarot (Lévi, Christian, 'Papus' etc.); but they are of course older than the 19th century, and may be found printed on cards belonging to very early packs. I am aware that some modern esotericals have set out the correspondences differently; and this they are perfectly welcome to do. These equivalences pertain to no exact science (such as the esotericals dream of), but to a more interesting though also more elusive thing — namely poetic fitness. Only, in such popular storehouses of wisdom, the 'corrupt' traditional version may be the richer and the more enduring — as our fable implies; and in fact the conventional symbolisations fall more naturally than the 'esoteric' ones, just as the old designs are finer than those of Miss Pamela Smith and Lady Harris — or even the quite fascinating reconstructions of Oswald Wirth. The present writer is neither occultist nor spiritualist, but a philosopher who believes in the revivification of the Idea (that poor sleeping princess, today entombed in the briar-thickets of universities) through her true guardian, the Symbol — the Spirit of Poetry, the Tarot Fool.

LE MAT

0 The Fool

The Fool is often placed at the conclusion of the Tarot — Court de Gébelin remarks pessimistically 'The game of life is played between a mountebank and a madman'

— but it seems equally appropriate to see him as its commencement. He is the 'Joker' of our ordinary playing-cards — the Origin and the End, the Zero and the Infinite, the Void before Creation and the Repose of the Seventh Day. He is the Genesis or Embryo, which is also the Genus — as the twelve Cards which follow him are the years of Childhood, and the nine after the great Break of the 'Hanged Man' are those of Adolescence (the nine germination-years of the mature self). The first thirteen Cards of the Tarot (by this reckoning) are *human* symbols, the remaining nine are *cosmic* ones. The Fool is pure Contingency, Impulse completely undetermined and free as air, both Will and Destiny and neither: he is aboriginal Chaos, primary Matter in which the dry and the earthy have not yet been parted from the wet and the oceanic. He is the traveller who tosses up at every crossroads, and, because he has no goal, cannot lose his way; or one might say that of him the aphorism of Kafka is true, 'There is an end, but no way — what we call the way is a shilly-shallying'. In this sense he seems an allegory, not only of humanity, but of the Gypsy race itself. We meet him again in the Hanged Man — his reversed image, the reflection he throws on Time's stream. In this Card he pauses on the brink of that stream, looking not downward but backward — heedless of the drop in front of him — and his dog, like a fate, presses him from behind. In some versions the dog is a tiger or panther — the 'pard', it may be, of the fool Dionysus; and a crocodile (perhaps that of Egyptian mysteries) waits to devour him. Or again, the Fool may stand for such figures as Orestes and Cain — or in our own time Synge's Christy Mahon — in flight from that parricide which Freud has seen as the mainspring of the human advance. This Card is also called 'the Mate' (il Matto, the Mad).

LE BATELEUR

ı The Juggler

The Juggler is the first Card in order and sequence, whereas the Fool was before all order and sequence — as the End is before the Beginning; so that, in a certain view, odd numbers are even numbers and the even the odd (a difficulty which accounts, incidentally, for the varying systems of numbering the Tarot). This is the essence of Irony, and the Juggler is an ironic spirit; one might call him (and not the Fool) the 'Joker', but it is the Fool — the backward-looking 'Unconscious Memory' — who haunts him and exposes his trick. The Juggler is forward-looking: he is not a Creator *ex nihilo* — for he deals with existent materials laid out before him (in fact, with Tarot cups, daggers and coins and, in his hand, the wand or sceptre—emblems familiar in folklore as 'the four Treasures of Ireland'). You may call him in fact *Time* — that ambiguous character that conjures birds out of eggs, as it were rabbits out of hats. He is the impulse of Play — most primitive of conscious states, which first halts the wanderer in the sociable market-place. The Juggler wears a bright intelligent expression, unlike the unkempt and uncouth Fool; Man has seated himself, and is master of the situation. His figure is the spiral of Time, the hour-glass, here represented in the curve of his hat-brim and other parts of the design; with the diagonal of the table, this Card also reproduces the Hebrew letter *Aleph*. One hand is raised, holding a wand like a sun's ray, while the other points to the earth. The Juggler is Adam, who gives names to all the objects in the garden; he is *language* — the poet uttering the Word which brings *essences*, like soap-bubbles, out of the liquidity of *existence*; the shimmering Light of the first morning. His letter in the old Germanic Runes is *Fa* (letter of *Fire*) — a torch waved in the Void.

2 The High Priestess

In this Card, as we might anticipate, Woman appears. Man has now a job, and does not long remain alone. The High Priestess — vulgarly known as the *Papesse* or

LA PAPESSE

'Pope Joan'—is the *Moira* (Destiny) of the Greeks, who is before all particular and local divinities. If the Juggler is the magician, she represents the magic — or relational web — of Nature. She or her daughters — servants of the Temple — have a long history in the medical art; for the healer of the body is more ancient perhaps even than the priest (of Card five) — the healer of the soul —

[11]

and her benign mysteries are older than his sacrificial ones. She holds half-opened on her knee the Tora (of which Tarot is perhaps a variant) — the Book of the Law and Prescription. She is what Nietzsche and the Existentialists have called 'the spirit of seriousness', as the Juggler was the spirit of play. In other words, she is Space, the formative—as he was Time, the *transformer*. Everything about her suggests remoteness and mystery. Behind her is the Veil of the Temple studded with stars, she is crowned (in some variants) with the Full Moon, and she is attired in gauzy shimmering robes. This Card is as distinctly *watery* in feeling as the Juggler is bright and electric, and as the Fool was windy and wispy: for seriousness is the principle of *weight* and also of *wetness* in objects — the *Law* which opposes itself to the *Play* of irony and caprice, that the game may go on. The Priestess is the Hebrew *Beth* (an enclosing house); in Runic she is *Ur*, the primordial heaven, represented by a basin or container (under which symbol, however, she is assimilated to our next figure, the Empress — as Lilith, in the Genesis, is effaced by the more human Eve). Our playboy has come into contact with natural law; but he has not yet entered upon the responsibilities of marriage.

3 The Empress

The Empress is an altogether more flesh-and-blood person; with her we are for the first time on the Earth. The celestial Moon-Woman, the Virgin Diana, has merged into a terrestrial Corn-Woman or Fertility-Goddess — the Venus-Urania, the *Magna Mater* of Mediterranean cults. The Empress is fecundity; she is the flux of history or formed matter, as the Fool was that of prehistory and the formless; she is maternal and material Earth — the last of the physical 'elements' and first of the biological 'kingdoms' — the ending of the

III

L'IMPERATRICE

primitive Odyssey prior to the Virgilian founding of states. In her, the fruit of the Heavenly Tree — heavy with foreknowledge — has become conscious of its destiny as seed; but we are still in Eden — in a matriarchal world before the rise of Israel and the Classical culture, with their tense abstract *Will*. She is the matrix of civilisations, the whole Glory of the World, the *Being*

[13]

of Hegel's system, waiting to be activated by the *Nothing* — like a fertilising flood — of the pure ethical Idea. Her letter in the Hebrew is *Gimel* (which perhaps means the camel — the load-bearing, water-loaded animal). She is the drowsy ante-diluvian 'Saturnian Age' to which every later age looks back, the Mother-Imago of Freudian psychology. We may say that our first three characters were figures of carnival — a Fool, a Conjuror and a She-Pope; but now serious business has begun — play has become earnest.

4 The Emperor

Following the Empress we have the Emperor; our hero, the Fool, we take it, has won a great Queen, as in the Fairy Tales. She will reappear at the end of the series in the Card called the World — as the Queen of the World. And if the Empress is the great Mother, the Emperor is as clearly the archetypal Father. He is the Olympian Zeus, the Old Testament Jehovah, the 'Urizen' of William Blake; his sign is that of the planet Jupiter. Historically, he represents the coming of patriarchy from the East (Hebrews) and the North (Dorian Greeks), as the Priestess was Egypt and the Empress was the Creto-Aegean culture. He clasps his sceptre firmly in front of him, and the escutcheon — which the Empress raised protectively to her side — sits at his feet. His outline — an upright triangle surmounting a cross — is the opposite of the Hanged Man's. With him, one feels, the masculine Mind and Will have commenced their dominance in the world; in most versions he is shown in profile — expressing thrust and singleness of aim — and in some he is seated on a cubic stone, to indicate the cruel compelling weight of logic and the Ego. The Emperor's letter in Hebrew is *Daleth*, the

[14]

L'EMPEREUR

door — through which man enters into his kingdom
(Irish *Dair*, the kingly oak). In the Runic it is *Thorn* or
Thor — partly, no doubt, with the same signification,
but also because he is Thor the Thunderer, the opener
of heaven and earth; and his hieroglyph (a variant of
our letter D) is a hammer or axe. After the four elements, Life itself has begun; the Fool has found a
direction, Energy has become conscious.

LE PAPE

5 The Pope

If matter (or earthiness) began with the Empress, and
Life (or vegetativeness) with the Emperor, we may see
the first coming of Death (or creaturehood) in the next
Card — the Pope. In the Zodiac, which commences
with this Card, his sign is Aries, the sacrificial Ram. As

[16]

the High Priestess stood to the Juggler in the relation of Law to Impulse, so we might say that the Pope stands towards the Emperor as the Codifier to the Source of Power, or the Tutor or Guardian towards the Father. To put it differently, he is the Soul, as the Emperor was the Body. But this is to use Soul and Body in the paradoxical, specifically human, sense of the Classical European tradition; if we use them with their primary meanings of Energy and Form, Life and Death, we shall have to make the contrary identifications. For during the World-Era which begins with Greece—and (roughly) with this Card — the 'Soul' has meant the specific Form restricting the individual Energy of the Body; and in this sense the 'Pope' represents mortal man's discovery of himself, as the 'High Priestess' meant his first discovery of Nature. Men here are seen kneeling before their image, mitred Man. The corresponding letter in Hebrew is *He* (the breath) — the second vowel or 'mediator' between consonants in the name of God, Ja-Ve (as the Juggler's letter, Aleph, was the first). In Runic it is *Od* or *Or* (akin to *Wort*, the holy *Word*), the replica but opposite of the primary letter *Fa* — a *downward*-held torch. The Juggler and the Pope are those two eternal yet opposite media of Truth, the artist and the priest.

6 The Lover

It seems almost incongruous to see the 'Fall' of Eden in this amusing design, though in some reconstructions we are shown indeed two lovers, with — behind them — the famous Trees. At all events, with this Card, which leads off the second pentad, we pass from the hierarchical to the human—and even the moralising—sphere. We are no longer in Egypt, nor even in Crete, but in

VI

L 'AMOVREVX

cheerful prosaic Europe—in a world of allegories rather than archetypes. This is the Card, no longer of Civilisation or Order, but of a more mature thing — Society. The Great Goddess has given place to her sportive son, the 'little god'; the drifting Fool has become the wayward spirit of Folly. In the usual version here shown, we behold Youth torn between the rival attractions of

[18]

Wisdom and Pleasure — the one crowned with laurels, the other with flowers. It is clear enough that he is going to opt for Pleasure, as is suitable to his age; there will be enough about Wisdom later. This Card is in fact the Judgment of Paris. In the sign-world of the heavens, the 'Lover' stands under Taurus. The letter for Card six in Hebrew is *Vau* (a nail or hook — suggesting both an attachment and the equivocal idea of a 'catch'). V is the letter of Eve — the second consonant in the Divine Name. In the Irish alphabet it is perhaps *Saille*, the Willow — tree of enchantment (the serpentine letter S). In Runic it is *Rit*, the Rite — a rite which (whether sacred or profane) first confers *rights*; for humanity has now come of age. With this Card we have reached the fourth kingdom — the human — as the 'Pope' stood for the animal and the 'Emperor' for the plant world. We shall see that in Hebrew the letter R signifies not human right but divine judgment (Card twenty).

7 The Chariot

The Card called The Chariot is as clearly the symbol of War as the preceding one was that of Love. The child of Adam and Eve is Cain; *Amor*, as mystics have said, when reversed is *Roma* — the nursling of the she-wolf. The eternity of Marriage is an attempt, like the famous proof of Zeno, to halt Eros's dart — that arrow in flight which is historic Time, and its burden of 'generation and ruin'. War is the serpent in the flower of Sex; one thinks of W. B. Yeats's Leda, and the shudder in the loins which engenders burning Troy. This Card has in fact for its sign Leda's progeny, the Twins. Love is a search for the *Other*, and the *Other* of Life is Death; but this is not consciously realised till the thirteenth Card, after the great reversal of Love in the twelfth — the Hanged

VII

LE CHARIOT

Man. The charioteer wears on each shoulder a half-moon — signifying the power he abrogates to himself over Life and Death. In the restored Tarot of Wirth, his chariot is drawn not by horses but by sphinxes (a white and a dark steed), to show that he is not only a material but a mental conqueror — the Charioteer of Plato's allegory. For all that, he embodies ruthless power — the self-confident intellect. He is Will in action — whereas the Emperor was Will in statuesque repose, the archetypal idea of Will, the monarch by divine right; this Card stands to the fourth as does the sixth to the third. One may say also, he is the conquering sun of May. The corresponding letter in Hebrew is *Zain* (a weapon). In the Runic it is *Kun* or *Kon* (race, and also virility — root of *König*).

8 Justice

In Card seven, the youth who chose to follow Pleasure still found himself pulled this way and that. The number eight — because it divides and re-divides evenly — was called by the Pythagoreans the number of Justice. This figure — the conventional emblem of Justice — has a similar significance to the 'High Priestess' and the 'Pope': all three oppose rest to motion or passive reflection to vital force. The first represented *Wisdom*, the second *Understanding*, while 'Justice' stands for the abstract *Reason* — which tames the anarchic energies of Love and War, and opens, fittingly, the second septad. She is the Code, which every fruitful war establishes; as Troy's epic arose, in legend, from the sporting of Leda, so the Roman Republic was the continuation of Troy. In this Card we pass from primitive and mythological history, and the ground is laid for *spiritual* growth in the world — the subject of the second half of the Tarot system. Justice is shown seated, like the High Priestess, between two pillars or uprights — as though to emphasise that she is the balancer of opposites; if her prototype was Space — balancer of the mutations of Time — Justice or Reason is the balancer of all individual assertions of Will. The astrological sign is Cancer, termed in antiquity 'the Gate of Man'. Her letters in

Hebrew (*Heth*) and in Runic (*Halga* or *Hag-all*) coincide
— both meaning a *hedge* or sacred enclosure, like a
primitive sanctuary or place of assembly. The Runic H
is a star-shaped figure, also called the *All-Rune* or
perfect Rune — the key to all others.

VIIII

L'HERMITE

9 The Hermit

This Diogenes-like personage, holding up a lantern in his right hand while he rather infirmly grasps a staff in the other, is as immediately suggestive of Age as was 'the Lover' of Youth. He represents that isolation of the soul which is the penalty of any high material civilisation; he is not the solitude of the Heart — which is before and underneath all human relationships, and whose symbol is the Fool — but the solitude of the disillusioned Intellect, cut off from all human relationship. He is, like the Fool, a wanderer, but not like him looking backward — the rootless man in whom the instinctual fires have died, or been replaced by a cold 'inner light' in the cage of an abstract system. Historically, we are in the era of sad and noble sages — the Buddha or Marcus Aurelius (for the lawgivers — Lycurgus or Plato — come more appropriately under the preceding emblem). The Hebrew letter is *Teth*, a serpent or twisted fabric: the Hermit is, from the Hebraic point of view, the temptation of the subtle Grecian wisdom. In Runic the letter is *Not* or *Naut* (*night* — also *need*). The Zodiacal sign is the Lion — the traditional comrade of solitaries in deserts. The glory of Paganism has withered into Stoic wisdom, and we are on the eve of the great reversal of values. But the old world of Asia will continue to see in this phase (which we may perhaps identify with the 'Old Wise Man' of Jung) the ultimate of Truth; instead of going on to the Hanged Man it will return to his shadowy prototype, the Fool, as the nearest approximation to the superhuman.

10 The Wheel of Fortune

The title of the 'Wheel of Fortune' is one appellation — and derivation — of the Tarot (or 'Rota') itself, of which this is in fact the central Card. Unfortunately, none of the Cards has been delivered to us by 'the hands of Vice' in a more debased form. In Wirth's restored Tarot, the seven-spoked Wheel is surmounted by a sphinx, while the figures at the sides represent the god Anubis (ascending) and the monster Typhon (descending) —

X

LA ROUE·DE·FORTUNE

signifying, in the phrase of Blake, the Marriage of
Heaven and Hell, or the Eternal Recurrence of Nietzsche; but in the usual packs all three figures are dogs
and apes, the uppermost one being absurdly decked out
in royal insignia. (Or may there be a hint here of the
Meaninglessness which every secure and over-confident
Civilisation feels?) With the 'Wheel', man's self-dis-

covery is complete, as in the first pentad he made discovery of an outer world (so to speak, of his parents
and sponsors); the tenth Card is the *I*, the Runic *Is* (or
Being itself), the Hebrew *Yod* — the Divine Initial, out
of which (as the Cabbalists say) all the other letters are
composed. If the 'Hermit' was the thinker, the 'Wheel'
is the completed Thought—the Platonic world of Essences or Ideal Forms (reflected in the static world-order of
Classical Antiquity), knowing nothing yet of Will-in-
distance (*Wille-in-die-Ferne*) or direction in time. The
I is moreover the last letter of the old Irish alphabet,
associated with the tree of Death, the Yew; for the tenth
Card, like the Zero-Card, is both an end and a beginning. The Zodiacal sign is the Virgin — symbol of the
mature body, the perfectly reflecting consciousness,
awaiting the experience and self-transcendence of the
second decad. If 'the Lover' stood for *Choice* and
Temptation, this Card stands for *Chance* and Fate.

11 Strength

If the Wheel of Fortune reproduced the aimless — or
self-sufficient — wandering of the Fool, the Card called
Strength has many affinities with the Juggler; the outline
is nearly identical, and we recognise again the spiral-
shaped hat. It is a Card of renewed youth and legendary
feats; it stands under the sign of Mars. The figure — the
Virgin of Card ten — is not now a creator, but a tamer
of nature: Thought has grown stronger than the Thinker
— the *Lion* of Card nine — and closes his jaws with her
hands. (Or, as seems the better interpretation, she opens
them — gives voice and articulation to mute knowledge.)
Humanity has become hungry for the Marvellous — for
wisdom to declare itself as power, weakness as strength,
innocence as generative virtue. It is the world of the

LA FORCE

Pagan Empire — a world of prodigy-seeking, of obscure yearnings, of cruel contests and displays — the atmosphere of strangeness and terror familiar to us in the later verse of W. B. Yeats, with whose phases of Hunchback and Saint (in the system of *A Vision*) it approximately coincides. If with the last Card we were in the gambling casino, in this one we are in the Roman circus;

Chance leads to a new thing — Miracle. (In another view, it represents the first coming of Autumn, taming Summer's heat.) The 'staring virgin' has displaced Dionysus, the Juggler. We are reminded of that reverence for female chastity ('Una and the Lion') which is the counterpart of the veneration for male simplicity ('Parsifal'). This Card corresponds to the Runic A (*Ar*, the eagle); the Hebrew letter is *Kaph* — a wing or hand.

12 The Hanged Man

The Hanged Man — it is not difficult to see — is the Crucified God: the last card, so to speak, which the Old World had to play — the last of the gods or 'archetypes' of antiquity, who opened a new Era by accepting the human tragedy, an acceptance which meant a complete somersault or reversal of posture. Yet there is nothing shocking or tragical about this Card which depicts a youth in green jerkin suspended by one foot from a sort of rustic arch, shaped like the World-hieroglyph, Tau; only the position of the legs is cruciform — the youth is hanged by the foot and not the neck! We seem to be shown only a stage in the soul's journey—an *ordeal*, like the ordeals by which, in certain communities, the growing male attains recognition as a *person*. From this point onward, the soul is no longer a *player* on the earth; we are entering the years of schooling. The Cards which follow are cosmic symbols rather than human types; the character whose story we have followed through so many metamorphoses will now disappear from the scene, and his place be taken by supernatural or natural concepts—corresponding in fact to the pictures in our schoolbooks, from the angels and devils of medieval painting to the suns, stars and worlds of modern manuals of astronomy. The active virtues

LE·PENDU

will henceforward be less regarded than the patient ones; though that patience will lead to a hardening of the *Will*, hitherto undreamed of, with results both divine and devilish. The Hanged Man's head and torso form an inverted triangle — the cabbalistic sign for Water, as the Fool is associated with the sign for Air: the liquid — which, by its very passivity, turns into the density and resistance of the solid. His sign in the Zodiac is the Scales. The letter in Hebrew is *Lamed*, a goad or pointed instrument — in short, a discipline; in the Runic it is *Sig* or *Sal* — called the rune of Salvation — and its sign (Roman S) is the forked lightning. (Note: Court de Gébelin, with his century's prosaicality, thinks the 'Hanged Man' a total misconception; for him, this Card should represent Prudence — a man with one foot *suspended* in air, examining where to place it!)

13 Death

Though the Hanged Man was not shown as dying, it is clear that that was his significance, as he is followed immediately by Death — the fatal number thirteen. This Card is ominously left unnamed in the pack, but there is no doubt about him — he is the conventional skeleton with the scythe. He is surrounded by severed heads, hands and feet (all, be it noted, quite startlingly alive) — indeed, in his fury, he has cut off one of his own feet! It is thirteen that bursts the simple framework of the Year and the Day, and humbles the 'measure of all things' — Man. Thirteen is the Judas, the Bad Fairy at the Christening — the first intimation of the unknown and incalculable, of what Heidegger calls 'the possibility of impossibility'. For Death is not only the frontier between Time and Eternity, but that between the Future and the Past. At this stage the Present, from being a plane as limitless as sight itself, has narrowed to a point — the moment of self-division, of tension between the *will be* and the *has been*, between willing and having, the *thought* and the *thing*: the gulf which, in the Zero-Card, opened in front of the 'Fool' — the wanderer, looking backward to the country of childhood while Fate, in the shape of the dog, urged forward his

feet. Now, the dog — like the poodle in Faust's closet or
the Arabian Nights' genie in the bottle — has grown to
a grisly phantom. Historically, it is the barbarian mer-
cenary, ruling and ravaging in the Empire: the death of
the pagan physicality — before the birth of the Soul,
the discovery by man of his *Self*. In the Hebrew alphabet, 'Death' is the second of the 'Mother' consonants,

Memm (water — the element that caused the look of *reflection* in the last Card). In the Runic it is *Tyr*, the god who gives his name to the Zodiac (by corruption, '*Tier-Kreis*') and whose sign is an arrow—the old-Greek final consonant, T.

14 Time or Temperance

This gracious Card, showing an angel who pours water from one vase into another (or, it may be, mixes oil and water like the Etruscan augurs), is an apt image of Time — the ruling concept of the 3rd septad. Her association with 'Temperance' seems at first sight to be a vulgarisation; but it may have been wished to include her in a trio (along with 'Justice' and 'Strength') of personified Virtues — occuring at equal intervals and concluding their respective triads, like Aristotelian or Hegelian syntheses. Of the three maidens, however, Temperance alone is winged; and it may be not merely fanciful to see in her the Angel of the Resurrection — restoring measure and seasonal rhythm after every harvest of Death. She seems indeed to have strayed out of an angel-choir by some Florentine painter. The fourteenth Card is the Card of the Supernatural: of that strange period when man felt his life as a spray of water, tossed between invisible cups — of that world brought near to us in the poetry of Shelley, a world of subterranean rivers, caves and sunken light — the moment, as of early Spring, when we feel our being mysteriously loosened from its moorings. The Hebrew letter is *Nun*, the fish — symbol of Man in this era of history — the dweller in the Water (*Memm* of Card thirteen), as Time, the Life-spirit of Card one, is first discovered and known in the mirror of Death. The corresponding rune is *Bar* or *Bjork* — the rune of the *buried*, or hidden,

XIII

TEMPERANCE

things (perhaps merging with the idea of the *beginning* which attaches to the B — the first consonant of other alphabets). The Zodiacal sign is Scorpio, the Dragon who — in regeneration — is the Eagle (just as we have had the Lion and the Bull, associated with Cards nine and six, and shall meet the Angel — Aquarius — with Card eighteen). Card fourteen is the early Middle Age, after the chaos of the previous 'Dark' Age.

XV

LE DIABLE

15 The Devil

If 'Temperance' represented the Supernatural, the
'Devil' stands for the Infra-human — the comic mon-
strosity which haunted the later Middle Age: a cari-
catural Sphinx — goat-bodied, bat-winged and vulture-
clawed. 'He who would play the angel plays the beast'

— but equally the beast is the Cerberus who guards the World of Dreams. He is the first ugly manifestation of 'libido'—that anarchic positive force whose universality has been revealed by modern psychology, and who must be redeemed (in our Card twenty-one) to be shown as the genius of Life itself, the transformed Fairy Prince or Princess of fable. But for the Middle Age, Angel and Devil are still opposed, set apart in a static *Other* World: if the first stands for irresistible Order, the second typifies rebel Will, who holds the divided sexes in thrall. The Pagan Pantheon has become a 'Pandemonium', worshipped in secrecy by the degenerate Nature-cults, which yet hold the promise of a harmonised existence in time. The Zodiacal sign for this Card is the Archer — the lonely untamed savage and slayer, whose symbol is the male emblem. The letter in the Hebrew is *Samech* — the S which is at once the Serpent and the Spiral of Life. In the Runic, it is *Laf* (*life*, the returning leaf) — a mysterious rune which the old Germans scratched upon the graves. The Devil is the *Emperor* (Card four) — Will or Vegetative Life — repressed by Temperance, the *Empress* of Card three new born. Man is at the age of fifteen, after the vague poetic dreams which unfurl themselves at fourteen.

16 The Lightning-struck Tower

In this card the Devil of Card fifteen has really set things in motion! This falling Babel-Tower represents the necessary defeat of human action and conscious planning by the Incalculable Factor—a defeat supremely exemplified by the failure of the Crusades and the whole great moral and rational synthesis of the Middle Age. It also represents the blind Fate which — in the shape of new state-persecutions — struck so many races

LA MAISON DIEV

and individuals in this epoch. After this stage the self, as it were, sinks in upon itself. Thought becomes introspective, and action, though increasingly agitated, mechanical; the astronomical backcloth is vastly extended, and dwarfs the human (and even superhuman) actors. In the Cards that follow the sixteenth, we are no longer on Earth, in Heaven or Hell, but in the Universe.

[36]

If the sixth Card was the Fall, the sixteenth is a greater, indeed nobler, Fall — that of Lucifer rather than Adam — a disruption through intellectual more than sensual curiosity, as signified in the term *La Maison Dieu*. But the upsetting of 'the best-laid plans' has in it cosmic irony as well as human tragedy; and this sensational Card, depicting a sort of archetypal 'Blitz', is extremely amusing. In the primitive Runic, this stage is hardly yet distinguished from the preceding one; we find no separate rune. The Hebrew letter is *Ayin* (the eye) — of which the shape is reproduced in the falling figure on the left. The Zodiacal sign is Capricorn, symbol of discord, 'the Gate of the Gods'. In the individual life, disillusions and stresses have begun.

17 The Star

The Card called 'The Star' is like a variant of 'Time', only that the figure is here no angel but a naked maiden, who empties *both* her vessels — the one into a lake, the other upon the ground. She rests on one knee at the water's edge, amidst an undulating landscape crowned with a flowering bush, on which a bird or butterfly has alighted. The sky is almost entirely filled by eight stars, one of them of remarkable effulgency. This is a card of Evening — or, what is the same thing, of Science and Enlightenment: we are in the era of 'Newton, Bacon and Locke' — the world not merely of Time but of Space. Man seeks to live according to Nature, and to merge in their primary elements his fevered 'blood and clay'; his life is no longer (as in Card fourteen) tossed to and fro by gusty impulse, but is allowed to trickle — pleasantly or beneficently — drop by drop. It seems like an illustration in an edifying romance or textbook of anthropology, where the primitive is chaste and the

XVII

L'ETOILE

soul is a bird- or butterfly-myth. This Card is associated
with the planet Mercury — the urbane god; but the
bright star is understood to be the Dog-Star Sirius,
identified by the Egyptians with the beneficent Hermes,
and who (perhaps) appears in the next Card as the
baying dog between the Moon and Cancer. Seventeen
is the Card of Hope, as eighteen is the Card of Despair.

The letter in Hebrew is *Phe*, the mouth. In the Runic, it is *Man* — the symbol of perfected man, with arms upraised.

18 The Moon

If 'the Star' was Evening, 'the Moon' is certainly Night. This might almost be called a surrealist picture — as Time was a Botticelli angel, and the Devil was a detail out of Hieronymus Bosch, and the Tower was a battle-scene, and the Star was a landscape-painting; it expresses solitude and dread. Two squat towers guard some secret fastness on an inhospitable coast; in the middle distance, a dog and a wolf at once bay the moon and bar the way in and out (the dog — associated with Hecate, goddess of the moon and of the underworld), while a lobster or some other marine horror crawls out of the deep onto the shore. The Moon does not so much shine as shed leprous flakes of light — in some versions they are blood-drops. It is the 'waning moon' of Coleridge's famous lines—with, below her, the Pillars of Hercules, the limits of the ancient world. Our spirit feels hemmed in between those twin towers-in-arms, as between two absolutes or logical alternatives; and the relativism which is subtly-adaptive life appears, as yet, only in the ignoble guise of 'compromise'. With this Card we know at once where we are; it is the age of Power-ideology and the Guilt-complex — of *The Castle* and *The Beast from the Abyss*—the fable, not of Grimm (like 'the Fool') nor of Aesop (like 'Strength'), but of Kafka. This is the obverse and conclusion of the Era of Enlightenment, as 'the Devil' was the flaw in the Era of Faith; Knowledge calls up dread of the Irrational, as Supernaturalism (Card fourteen) ends in deformation of the Natural. The Zodiacal sign is Aquarius — water

LA LUNE

being associated with reason's illusion of Matter, and also (in another aspect) with the 'Unconscious'. The letter in the Hebrew is *Tsaddi*. In the Runic it is *Yrr* (chaos or *error*); this rune is in fact the preceding one — the sign of Man (and of 'humanism') — turned upside down.

XVIII

LE·SOLEIL

19 The Sun

In this Card we have a feeling of Morning; it is a simple expression of joy and regained innocence, in the manner of William Blake. Two children are playing outside a walled enclosure; or, as in some variants, a child or youth — on horseback and carrying a flag — rides away

[41]

from an enclosed garden. For a moment those restricting limits are left behind; man's load of memory seems to have fallen from him, as Bunyan's Christian was freed from the pilgrim's wallet of his sins. As 'the Star' symbolised the Reason and 'the Moon' the Irrational, so 'the Sun' is the true Super-rational — the freedom of the harmonised personality. It is the moment of renovation expressed in the modern dream of untrammelled 'self-expression': half-delusive — like the great experiment of the New World, for history cannot be merely annulled but must be integrated in man's total life. This Card is under the sign of the Fishes — the sign of the whole Era, as the next Era will be dominated by the Water-Carrier; for the Unconscious of Card eighteen, which came as the experience of despair, will be recognised as man's truest hope. 'The Sun' (Pisces) stands in fact to 'the Moon' (Aquarius) as did 'Time' (Scorpio) to 'Death' (element of Water) — expressing birth or renewal out of chaos. The corresponding letter in Hebrew is *Quoph*. In Runic it is *Eh*, or 'marriage', and its form is the reversal of the letter *Not*; for with the nineteenth Card the connections between surface and depth that were severed in the ninth are re-established.

20 The Last Judgment

The Judgment is the Card of the Future. It represents the secret aim of humanity, expressed in a hundred myths, to justify the Past — and so bring it to life: which may at last annul the Medusa-like doom of the Present to become petrified as Past, and conquer (in that instant of perfected intuitive perception) the traitor of Card thirteen — the enemy Death. A man, a woman and a youth are here shown arising from the tomb, in attitudes of piety. The Judgment is the world-view of the

LE · JUGEMENT

artist-philosopher, which opens all 'tombs' and can see the Form hidden under all Accidents; a sage who — seeking to change nothing — will not be tempted to action, but perceiving that the world is good will grant it (and be granted in return) a *Nunc Dimittis*. He is to be distinguished from the Hermit of Card nine, who refuses the world and action because they are evil, and so cannot cease to wander — not recognising the Lord: for the Medusa of Death can be slain only by holding up to it the mirrors of experience and acceptance. The Judgment concludes the work which the Juggler commenced, of turning all existence to essence, evoking consciousness out of unconsciousness by the power of the Word, and revealing the logical syntax of Being. This Card stands under Saturn—at once Demon (Satan) and Saviour (Soter). It is the Hebrew *Resh*, the head: the Runic *Gibur*, the last and holiest letter — a cross with the two arms (but not the central stroke) bent at right angles, pointing to heaven and to earth.

2) The World

'The World' is a metaphysical phase, which is the reason why (like 'the Fool') it has no equivalent in the primitive runes. This nude maiden — a Kali dancing down the world — is Eternity, as the Fool was Infinity, the Eckhartian 'Abyss of Godhead': her feet — like the Hanged Man's, but unbound and in movement — form a cross. She is the same female that we met with in 'Time' and 'the Star' — in fact, in the third Card of almost all the triads: only that here she synthesises the two entire decads of our series — the twin opposites of innocence and experience, instinct and reason, day and night, Nature and the Divine — she is the eternal morning of him who, instead of bending joy to his will, kisses it as it flies. The bower which framed the Hanged Man has become an ellipse formed by a flower-studded garland, around which are gathered the four symbolic creatures of the Apocalypse — the four quarters of the Cherub in Hebrew mysticism — corresponding with the four pentads of the series. She is the alchemists' 'Quintessence' — as much of fire as of earth, as much of air

LE·MONDE

as water — the *concrete actuality* which is at once ideal
and material, as the Fool was *pure potentiality*: she,
the bride, is Cosmos as he was Chaos — she is the
attained *Sophia*, or Wisdom, of him who 'persists in his
folly'. In her, in Nietzsche's words, all spirit has become
raiment and all body a dancer. Her letter is *Tau*, last
letter of the Hebrew and early Greek alphabets, for the

penultimate *Shin* (third of the 'Mothers') is usually given to the Fool — whose place, we saw, is indeterminate, and may be seen as fitly before the omega as before the alpha. (In a sense, he is the perpetual alternative and last temptation: the Antichrist who is prophesied.) Her sign in the heavens is the Sun (feminine in the Irish and German), as her servant the Priestess's was the Moon. (Note: If, as we think, the High Priestess is Phase fifteen of the Yeatsian system, the World is perhaps Phase twelve, 'the Hero's Crescent').